Travelling with Cancer

Marianne Stevens

A catalogue record for this book is available from the National Library of Australia

Copyright © 2018 Marianne Stevens
All rights reserved.
ISBN-13: 978-1-876922-93-1

Produced by Linellen Press
265 Boomerang Road
Oldbury Western Australia
www.linellenpress.com.au

Dedication

To my very patient and supportive husband, Peter; my oncologist, Prof Arlene Chan and my empathetic neighbours. I owe you all a debt of gratitude.

Contents

Dedication iii

Contents v

Acknowledgments vii

Chapter one 1

Chapter Two 11

Chapter Three 14

Chapter Four 18

Chapter Five 20

Chapter Six 22

Chapter Seven 23

Chapter Eight 26

Chapter Nine 28

Chapter Ten 32

About the Author 44

Acknowledgments

Thanks to Alison, my nursing friend, who suggested I write this book to encourage other breast cancer patients.

Chapter one

'Are you really sure you have cancer?' a friend asked me just the other day. 'Only you look so well and are so positive. No one would guess there was anything wrong with you!'

'Unfortunately yes, I have secondary cancer, in other words its in my bones, pelvis, and spine.' I replied. 'It is what is termed 'metastatic cancer.'

I am a great believer in the old saying *'Laugh and the whole world laughs with you. Cry and you cry alone.'* I try and live as if this diagnosis was just a minor irritation. Side effects can come almost without warning — all medication has side effects and some worse than others. The most important thing is that I have a good quality of life and am still here! It's not a good feeling to know you have metastases (secondaries) in your body but it's not something I worry about on a daily basis.

My journey with cancer actually started back in 1986 when I noticed a small lump in my left breast. I always checked myself in the shower, which is how I found it. It felt like a small, hard frozen pea. (you can try doing that yourself so you know what it feels like). Later that morning I joined my friends at coffee break where I worked as a medical secretary in the Middlesex Hospital in London. When I explained to them about the lump I had found, the general consensus was that it was probably nothing but wise to get it checked. I had a very busy job in the hospital, working for two urologists and I enjoyed it very much. Little did I know that being there might have saved my life; I was in the right place at the right time! I also had worked in oncology in Canberra in the early 80s so knew not to put my head in the sand! It's a very natural reaction to do that and hope it might go away.

Peter and I were posted to Canberra in 1981 as he was asked to do a desk job there, on loan to the Royal Australian Navy. Reluctantly I agreed, as I wasn't sure about leaving our beautiful old house and had a sinking feeling my husband would want to stay in Australia. However, the funniest thing happened. I just loved Australia, everything about it from the easier lifestyle, the wonderful climate (yes even in Canberra!) and the amazing wildlife and I didn't want to go back to England!

*****

One of the saddest things we have had to do during our move was we had to give away our lovely golden Labrador, *'Tui'* as we would have had to put her into quarantine in Australia for 6 months and the same on our return to England. We just didn't think it was fair. No one in the family would look after her for us for 2½ years. We had her from a puppy and she was 6 when we gave her away. She went to a family who sent us photos so she had a good life in their care.

We had a wonderful 2½ years in Canberra and I enjoyed working in both the Radiology and the Oncology departments of the hospital there. It was where I first learnt about breast cancer. The nurses had found a way of conserving patients' hair and even beards, by putting ice cubes in shower caps; the earliest example of what is now known as the cold cap treatment. One very angry man came to the desk where I was on duty and was very difficult to deal with. However, once he had learnt that the staff could probably save his beard, he calmed down. I still remember one beautiful young woman, who was the wife of a local GP. She always dressed beautifully and was made up impeccably during her chemotherapy treatments. When I found I had breast cancer, she was a role model for me to follow. Years later I rang the GP up and told him how she had helped me and he was very touched. I decided that if I looked smart and was made-up, then I was ready to face the world.

Just 3 years after our return to the UK, on a Friday morning whilst showering, I found a lump in my left breast. I rang up my GP's surgery near our home in Somerset, where we would be spending the weekend. (This was over 3 hours' drive from London). I asked for an appointment the next day, but was very nearly put off when the receptionists were very unhelpful. Here I was, quite a sensible medical secretary who hardly ever darkened the doctor's door, asking for an appointment on a Saturday morning! Surely it was obvious it was important. This is one of the worst things patients often have to negotiate — the jail-like door of the doctor's room! How many women would have failed to be assertive enough? I came close to it. These women (and I am afraid they are nearly always female) often have too much power. They asked me if it was 'urgent' and how was I to know if my lump was cancerous or not? I nearly wavered. 'Yes' I said firmly, 'It is urgent.'

When I entered the GP's room in Crewkerne the next morning, I started off with '*It's probably nothing.*' My concerned GP said he had heard of '*probably nothings before*' but he took it seriously. After careful examination, he said there was definitely a lump there and we considered what would be the best course of action, as I worked in London during the week. I asked him for a letter of referral to give to one of the surgeons I worked for at the hospital and I would take it from there.

Monday morning was busy as usual. One of the urological specialists I worked for was doing a ward round, surrounded by eager medical students and fawning nurses. When he had finished, I cornered him on his return to my office. I said I had a breast lump and could he recommend anyone for me to see?

He laughed. *'Breast lumps are like Irish barmaids. They are all innocent until you take them out and prove otherwise!'* which was very funny and of course totally inappropriate in these PC days! He then suggested I call up the breast surgeon, John Scurr, who worked in the same building and see him; which was speedily arranged for that afternoon.

Mr Scurr (in the UK surgeons are called 'Mr or Ms whereas physicians are titled Doctor) took a biopsy and I was booked into our sister hospital, UCH, later that week and would be first on the list on the Friday morning — a week to the day I found it. I couldn't have had better treatment if I had paid to go privately. Sadly so many women have been put off by their doctors and not taken seriously. I was so lucky. Oddly enough, I wasn't too worried about the outcome; I just felt everything would be fine. The morning of the operation I worked as usual and then walked up to UCH, which was close by and was admitted. In fact looking back, I was quite nonchalant. A strange co-incidence was that my paternal grandmother had been a nurse there at the beginning of the 20th century, in their radiology department. Perhaps her ghost was looking down at me? I wasn't to know then that my grandmother 's genetic pattern had a vital role in my health. I have a lovely photo of her in her Edwardian nurse's uniform. In those days, it was unknown that the breast cancer gene could travel down the paternal line.

When I woke up in the recovery room, I was told that I had a small tumour and that my surgeon, John Scurr, would ring Peter, my husband. He had removed the tumour and suggested I see the medical oncologist for further treatment. Peter was obviously quite worried but reassured when he saw me looking quite cheerful that evening. Having spoken to the surgeon I think that helped him enormously. My tumour was described as *'a ductal cell carcinoma measuring about 2 cms with some lymphatic involvement."*

The following day I had a visit from the specialist I worked for and he looked frightfully remorseful and embarrassed after his joke about Irish barmaids! He was a very good-looking man and the other patients were all dying to know who he was as soon as he left! I could see their curious stares whilst he was talking to me! They were all quite envious when I said I worked for him.

I only had to stay in hospital for a couple of days after my lumpectomy. This was the removal of the lump and not a full mastectomy, which would have involved removing the whole breast. I talked to Mr Worth, the surgeon I worked for, about the psychological effects of a mastectomy on a woman and why many of us preferred to have a lumpectomy. He was quite taken aback as I don't think he had ever thought about it when working as a general surgeon. He said they just routinely did mastectomies. Perhaps I focused his mind on an alternative, which would not be a bad thing. When I looked at the site of the operation, there was only a small 'dent' in my left breast.

Whilst on the ward, the patient next to me told me she had noticed her breast lump eight months beforehand and was particularly worried, as her mother had recently died from breast cancer. She had been to the GP and he practically told her she was a hypochondriac and hysterical. The ignorant man didn't even check if there was a hereditary factor there. Now all these months later, she was in a dreadful state, crying and shaking. I tried to reassure her as I told her about one of our own patients who had MS and also breast cancer. As I said to her, we only have one disease to worry about. I was so shocked and upset when about a year later I found out she had died, and this was a case of a doctor burying his own patient. If that GP had been alert he would have sent her off for investigation immediately. In those days, far too many women died needlessly because of the poor behaviour of their doctors. If she had been treated when she first went to that GP, she would have had a pretty good chance of recovery. Of course poor doctors get away with things far too often. I felt so angry on her behalf; children left without a mother, which could have been avoided.

Once you have cancer, you become part of the system and an appointment with the oncologist followed. Dr Margaret Spittle was very well known and according to her, I was having the most up-to-date treatment. Over 30 years later I have had no reason to doubt her. My regime was the drug Tamoxifen taken daily (which I had for ten years), plus radiotherapy for 5 weeks followed by chemotherapy for 6 months. I had Cyclophosamide, Vincristine and Methotrexate.

The timing of my cancer operation couldn't have been worse. It was mid-July, the summer in England. It was a favourite cousin's wedding (she had been the flower girl at our own nuptials) and our two teenage daughters were breaking up for the long summer holidays that week. Thankfully, a great friend, Anna Drinkall, picked up the girls and took them home to her house in Yorkshire for a few days. Sadly we missed my cousin's wedding, but I will always remember the date!

During this time, and quite by chance, my husband Peter, a naval officer and helicopter pilot, had been allocated a desk job at the Admiralty in central London. We had rented a small apartment in Dolphin Square in London, which became an absolute haven during my treatment. Dolphin Square was a large block of apartments built just before WW2 and the buildings encircled attractive gardens in the middle. In the basement were housed a beautiful swimming pool, squash courts, a restaurant and a convenience store as well as a launderette. It was very warm and cosy; the central heating provided by excess heat from the nearby power station on the River Thames. It was only available to rent to those who worked uncertain hours including actors, politicians and service personnel. We were extremely lucky to get an apartment there. It had quite a colourful history, which we didn't know about until many years later. Jeffrey

Archer, the author, played squash there and I often recognised the odd MP or two. It was very safe and secure with hall porters in each block. These blocks were named after naval personalities and ours was 'Nelson House.'

I felt nauseous but never actually vomited with the chemotherapy and the radiotherapy seemed to have no effect, apart from skin changes. I was so fortunate not to lose my hair either. I reckoned I had an hour's grace before I could smell the awful chemicals in my nostrils and would feel a bit faint. I lost weight, which I was quite pleased about!

There is always a silver lining!

Radiotherapy is painless and the patient just has to lie still for about 10 to 15 minutes, whilst the radiation technicians retreat out of the room and the machine takes over; they keep a good eye on you from a window. Adjuvant radiation is used to shrink the cancer and to stop the growth of other cells. Then it's all over! Chemotherapy took longer and before treatment, patients have to have a blood test to make sure their white cell count is high enough to cope with it. I was fortunate not to have any problems with my blood count. I had an IV drip inserted into my hand and I found the chemo not too bad, and felt just a bit nauseous and very tired for a day or two afterwards. Everyone is different in how they react to treatment. I also found working throughout kept my mind off the illness and psychologically it was the best outcome.

At weekends we went home to our house in the country, which was on the border of Somerset and Dorset. On Saturday mornings we fetched the girls home from school where they weekly boarded. Victoria was in Sherborne and Claire a bit further away near Blandford. We had a huge garden to maintain and were also renovating our beautiful Queen Anne house. (It was built in 1710)

We had a very hectic schedule! My parents had recently relocated from Surrey to be near us in Dorset but my mother had been diagnosed with bi-polar disease and we were very worried about her. We unfortunately didn't have much time to see them. The lawns took nearly four hours to mow and we totally re-wired and re-plumbed the house. In the UK you can do that, but the work has to be assessed and certified afterwards. Thankfully, our wonderful neighbours in the village of Misterton were a great help and the girls proved to be dab hands at cooking. It is often stated that stress can cause cancer. I have no idea whether it does or not but we had a very busy life and I did stress about my mother. I could manage working in London, having treatment, and also doing the household chores but my mother's illness was one thing too much. Thankfully friends and neighbours were great, as I had no help from family apart from our two daughters. I was so pleased I had let them loose in the kitchen when they were small and they could both cook. My neighbours also prayed for me in our little village church just nearby and their support buoyed me up tremendously. My mother was a constant worry until by some miracle, she was put on Lithium and she was back to being the mother I remembered. Before this happened she had rung us in the middle of the night saying she had killed my father! Well, he was a difficult man so we did wonder if it was true or not! We tried to call but he didn't answer, so we had to dash down in the car to check if he was still alive or not! He very apologetically answered the door to us, but it was a very stressful time.

The oncology department at the Middlesex Hospital was very dowdy, overcrowded and in a poor state. It was in sharp contrast to the very 'PC' HIV department (in other words AIDS), which Princess Diana opened. They even had a microwave installed. Sadly, cancer was a poor relation. I have no issue with the HIV department being modernised, but far more patients were being treated for cancer and it seemed grossly unfair. The hospital has since been demolished but the 'listed' beautiful chapel still remains.

On the day of Prince Andrew and Sarah Ferguson's wedding, I was being marked up with gentian violet ready for my radiotherapy. I think the staff had a better day than I had as every so often they would race to the TV screen and come back telling me what was happening! This gentian violet tainted clothes and bras so I always chose a dark coloured bra and dark clothing when I went for the treatment. Nowadays they use a different type of marker.

The old linear accelerators (radiotherapy machines) were very different to what we have now in our up to date radiation oncology departments They would call me and I dashed down there in my lunch break. It didn't take very long thankfully. When it came to chemotherapy treatment, I asked to have it as late as possible on a Friday afternoon so that I could go home and relax. I would be pretty knocked out for a day but was well enough to go to work on Mondays. I reckoned I had an hour before being overcome with the nauseous feeling and chemical smell from the chemo. I nearly fainted on the tube one day so Peter came to pick me up with the car instead. The Middlesex Hospital had the smallest car park and it was very difficult for him to do this. He had to sit in the car and double-park until I emerged. Somehow we managed. Parking was so bad that one of the surgeons I worked for used a bike to get to the other hospitals where he operated.

After my treatment I went back to the apartment and collapsed into bed, hardly moving all night. Thankfully I never actually vomited. I also didn't lose my hair although one of the nurses told me that the patient before me, having the same treatment, lost all hers, so I was very fortunate! Tamoxifen gave me an early menopause and I was probably close to having it anyway at age 45. At nights I would often be drenched in sweat from that together with the chemo treatment. Thankfully we had two single beds there so I didn't disturb Peter. Life was easy as I could do the washing in the basement launderette and buy items in the grocery store. It was very welcome in the winter as there was no need to venture outside.

I tried to be very blasé about my treatment so that the girls wouldn't be worried. At the time they were teenagers and one day one of them asked if she could bring a friend home for the weekend. I said of course but she would have to catch the train down to our village (the station was 5 mins walk from our house) because I had to lie down on the back seat all the way from London to Somerset, which was a three-hour journey. I had a panicked phone call from the girl's mother asking if it was all right for her daughter to come down as she heard I had cancer. I said it was fine; I just had to rest for the first day! The girls, as I had hoped, were very nonchalant about it! People often had odd ideas about cancer. You find out who are your real friends when going through a traumatic period in your life. The people you least expect seemed to be helpful and I was very hurt that my brother in law and his wife didn't contact me for a month. I later found out that Peter's mother had told them we didn't want it known and not to get in touch! That was an absolute untruth as I had always very open about it. I think the problem was with her as she called it *'The Big C'* in hushed tones! No wonder she was frightened as she had an old-fashioned attitude to it. Nowadays so many people who get cancer are able to live pretty good lives for a long time and it's not the death sentence it used to be. Research has been amazing in recent years and the oncologists are trying new drugs and treatments all the time. People ask me if I am cured and I say I never will be but I am being kept alive and so far living with metastatic cancer has been fine. I try and not worry about the side effects when I can look out of the window and see a beautiful blue sky and flowers. Nobody looking at me would think I had a serious illness! The side effects are a minor issue.

Chapter Two

Back in 1986, we had booked a summer holiday in the Greek Islands, long before my diagnosis. I managed to change the date slightly so I could fit in my radiotherapy sessions before we went. I had the first of the scheduled chemo treatments and completed the 6 weeks of radiotherapy before we flew to Skiathos for two weeks.

I can remember standing in what was no more than a hot tin shed waiting for the ferry after we landed in Skiathos; (Skopelos doesn't have an airport). We were then transported to Skopelos. Co-incidentally, just before I went under the anaesthetic in the Middlesex hospital theatre for my operation, I had been chatting to the Greek-born anaesthetist and he said how lovely Skopelos was and that usually only Greeks knew about it. He was right Skopelos was beautiful but is now known by so many people as the island where the first *Mama Mia* movie was filmed and sadly it is bound to lose its charm.

I sat on board the ferry for the short journey without moving a muscle, as I was exhausted. When we arrived at our hotel I slept for the first two days. We were fortunate that a school-friend of our elder daughter was also staying on the island with her parents and they took the girls to their hotel for the weekend. We had chosen half-board which was a blessing, as I didn't feel like venturing out very often for meals at night. Because of the strong radiotherapy in those days, I had a very sensitive area around the operation site and when I bathed in salty seawater, it was very painful. Peter had a good idea and we bathed it with bottled water when I came out of the sea. He also put up an umbrella to shade me from the sun and I wore factor 50 sunscreen. I had a very 'tanned' looking area in that spot for a couple of years. I had heard some old wives tales that I wouldn't be able to go swimming. I thankfully had advice from an oncologist friend, Dr Ken Sunderland in Canberra, who said it was rubbish. You tend to get much unwanted advice and people sending you 'miracle' cures when you let them know you have cancer. Of course they are well meaning but I just thanked them and went with what my oncologist suggested. The worst case was a friend in New Zealand who spent a fortune, which she didn't have, on an expensive regime of Vitamin C injections; money down the drain. If there is a miracle cure, surely someone like Steve Jobs would have taken that option. In fact everyone I know who went with 'natural cures' and didn't go down the accepted medical way, has died. It is fine to do both really i.e. eat sensibly with plenty of fresh fruit and vegetables, cut down on alcohol and do exercise. The latter is very important as chemotherapy is supposed to work better when you exercise. I find aqua aerobics very beneficial and it's whatever suits you.

Our daughters were champing at the bit whilst on the island and were itching to go off on their own to a nightclub. We refused to let them, as they were quite young. However, I found out in later years they had climbed out of the bedroom window and gone there with the hotel owner's son!! So glad I didn't know that at the time; stress I didn't need! It was a wonderful holiday and we managed to get out and about, walking around the pretty island and even hired a scooter a few times. The Greeks love it when you inspect their kitchens and see what is going to be on the menu that night. The beaches tended to be stony but the sea was absolutely beautiful. By the end of the holiday I felt much stronger and fitter.

After the holiday, I returned to work at the Middlesex Hospital and everyone was very supportive. I had a bit of a convoluted walk from my office to where we held the outpatient clinic. The patients' notes were already there but I had to carry them back with me to my office. The surgeon (with the Irish joke!) very kindly carried them for me, which was quite something as in those days doctors were like 'Tin Gods' and no other specialist would have been seen dead carrying notes for his secretary! We had a lovely ward clerk who would answer my phone when I was having treatment. I had landed this job, which was particularly hectic because there had been a gap of three months without a secretary. In my small, cramped office, there were piles of patients' notes awaiting discharge summaries and this was on top of typing all the clinic letters. The GPs were getting tetchy that they hadn't heard about the operations performed on their patients and the Registrar (junior doctor) whose job it was to dictate these was also new. He didn't know the patients; so I decided on a plan to try and sort them out. He dictated a very short letter to each GP based on what he read in the notes. It wasn't ideal but better than nothing. At the same time, notes would be required for either a follow-up appointment or for other clinics the patient might be attending. It was quite a nightmare to try and keep up to date with them. The Medical Records department was also housed in a different building, so to get urgent notes I would have to go down three flights of stairs, cross over the road and request the notes which then had to be found in their sprawling building. Sometimes it would be very cold or even raining so no wonder the hospital was eventually knocked down!

Chapter Three

When I had my operation, the surgeon suggested to Peter that with my diagnosis, our rather stressful lifestyle might not be a good idea. We had been discussing over the past few months whether to stay in England or return to New Zealand where we had lived for two years in 1970-72. We loved the lifestyle over there and although we had a beautiful old house and the children were at good schools, we felt we weren't getting enough out of life. I have always been slightly psychic, and I had a feeling long before I had my diagnosis, that we would be planning to do something like move overseas and I would have a problem which might put paid to our plans. To us, life 'down under' was much more relaxed and carefree.

The house in Somerset

Peter had taught the New Zealander pilots to fly a particular helicopter when we were stationed in Auckland in the early 70s and now he was asked to return there to join a team investigating the purchase of a more up-to-date model. It was something we were very keen to do but I worried that having breast cancer would stop that. Usually migrants had to wait for 5 years to check if they were free from disease etc. We didn't have that time up our sleeve as you had to be under a certain age as well. It would also be perfect timing as he was due to retire from the Royal Navy about the same time.

I asked Dr. Spittle a hypothetical question about us going to NZ and coincidentally she knew the person who did the medicals for New Zealand House. I asked her to check what the doctor thought as she could discuss my medical condition with him. He concluded that there was no problem and so we were free to go, after completing the medical check-up. This was now autumn 1987 and we had a farewell dinner with family in a Chinese restaurant in Pimlico near our Dolphin Square apartment. We then packed up our belongings in London and driven back down to Somerset. We had tried very hard to rent our house out but being three hours from London, it was impossible. We had some very odd people who wanted to rent it and an old house can't be left unoccupied, as things tend to go wrong with them. For instance we had a lead gulley in our roof and snow would often settle there and had caused a leak in the past.

Back in 1981-83 whilst on our posting to Canberra, Australia, we had a very strange tenant in the house during the two and a half years we were away. He was a man who wore shorts throughout the cold English winter and walked everywhere. He also had over 3000 books in the house. At one stage we found out from concerned neighbours that he had advertised our house as a small boarding school for boys! In fact he had a small number of boys living there and they caused some damage. One had managed to put a hole in the very thick old walls in the house and another had taken the motor mower apart which completely wrecked it. When we came to return to England, he refused to leave. He thought the house was big enough for all of us! Thankfully we had good agents who took it on themselves to remove him. He had left all his books behind which they managed to collect and the next thing we heard was that the tax authorities were looking for him and took the books in part payment!

During the summer of 1987, we had been invited to the RNAS Culdrose down in Cornwall for Air Day and considered whether to have a day or two away from packing up our house or not. In the end we decided to go which was fortuitous. I sat next to a man, Dougie Hale, who had founded *Flambards*, a theme park with a Victorian village and other attractions in nearby Helston. He had heard we were moving to New Zealand and asked what we were doing with our house? He probably had heard from our friend Jimmy James, the Captain of the base, that we had a lovely house. Anyway I just so happened to have a photo of it in my bag. I drew it out and handed it to Dougie to look at. His eyes lit up and he remarked that he and his wife had been looking for such a property for ages and if it was possible, his wife would come to look at it the next day. We agreed to this but said the house wouldn't be looking its best as the removalists would be there packing up! This didn't put them off and she came around to see the house. We then had an offer from Dougie to buy it but we loved the house so much we didn't want to sell it. We were much keener to rent it out so if New Zealand didn't work out, we could return. Dougie made a few more offers, each time being rebuffed. Finally the offer was so good we agreed to sell it.

We then had to rush around as everything in the house had to go as it was being sold and we were within days of leaving England. We had a few things, which were going into store, but the rest were accompanying us to New Zealand. We had earlier decided to leave things in our huge attic space but now it all had to go! As time was running out, we sent the girls up to London on the train ahead of us and we followed the next day. We had booked a few nights back in Dolphin Square in the hotel section of the building. As we walked tearfully down the drive in Misterton for the last time we both were quiet and very upset. We had the house for ten years and had lovingly restored it; it was a special home and hard to leave. We hoped New Zealand would make up for our loss. Wiping the tears away, we boarded the train for London and off to a new life overseas.

Chapter Four

The flight out was via Hong Kong where we spent a couple of days. When it rained, Claire was thrilled 'Warm rain!' she exclaimed. We arrived in Wellington in New Zealand towards the end of winter but the city was miserable looking. It just looked dismal with dreary buildings and to make matters worse we were booked into a very '*dated*' motel. For the first time in my life I sat on the bed, close to tears and wondered whether we should just pick up our bags and go back. I had never felt defeated before as I am a very optimistic person but I certainly wavered then. Of course now I am glad we stayed put, as we would never have ended up in Australia otherwise. We also made many wonderful friends in our four years' stint in New Zealand

Just before leaving the UK, I had arranged to have a genetic test. These were very new and I had to go to a temporary hut building in the Anthony Nolan part of St Mary Abbots Hospital where I was working at the time. It took over a year for the result to come through and I then found out I was carrying the BRCA 2 gene, inherited from my paternal grandmother. It was unknown then that the faulty gene could travel down the male line. This accounted for the fact that my grandmother had died of breast cancer, her sister, my great aunt, had had breast cancer but survived, and my father in later years would die from prostate cancer and my sister also had breast cancer. Another aunt had it and survived till she was in her 90s. This was all down through the male line and both my daughters have inherited the faulty gene.

Wellington changed dramatically in the years we spent there. It is now a vibrant and attractive city but deserves its reputation as a windy city. We bought a house with a stunning view of the harbour in a suburb called Khandallah. Wellington is very hilly and the houses are mainly of wooden construction as it lies on a fault line. The girls only had a year or two left at school so were enrolled into Marsden Collegiate in Karori. It was very much run on the lines of the English school they had been in. They both made very good friends there and were soon feeling at home.

I started work quite quickly and held a variety of jobs in the three and a half years we were there. After a certain length of time we obtained NZ citizenship. Peter was busy up in Auckland and only home at weekends as he was organising the 50th anniversary of the RNZN. At the same time he was looking for a job outside the Navy up in Auckland. None was forthcoming, but he was in touch with a recruitment agency in Sydney who sent him for an interview with Australia's largest Defence Company based in Canberra.

The girls had finished school and Claire didn't want to go to university sadly so I made sure she did a secretarial course as a backup, and Victoria did a short keyboard skills course. I told them they could earn more money 'temping' than waitressing if all else failed. Victoria did this before enrolling in a Hotel Management course in Melbourne.

Chapter Five

During this period I had annual check-ups and mammograms with the oncology department in Wellington. All seemed fine and I was still on Tamoxifen, which I took for ten years. I subsequently found out that Tamoxifen is thought to carry on safeguarding the patient for a year or two after ceasing it. I didn't have any side effects with Tamoxifen although some patients complain about weight gain.

I had no further symptoms or problems and we then moved across 'the ditch' to Australia for Peter to take up his new position. As we had lived there before, it was so easy for us to slot back into life in Canberra and I soon found a job with an obstetrician/gynaecologist. Victoria went to Melbourne where she enrolled in her hotel management course and Claire to Sydney where she worked for Delta Airlines. They would come home at odd times and we had a dear little mustard-coloured Mini Cooper they used whilst in Canberra. I enjoyed catching up with old friends there and loved Canberra's change of seasons. Spring is so pretty and of course there is the wonderful Floriade Festival then, and in the autumn the trees turn to rusty, golden tones. New house owners were always given a tree to plant years ago but unfortunately that has ceased. When I look around at the new housing estates here in Western Australia, I wish that applied here as the lack of trees is disappointing and there is just a sea of roofs.

We decided to buy our own house in Canberra, but there had been rumours that the company might move to Sydney. As we were assured that would not happen, we bought the house I had always loved, in Pearce. It was a pretty colonial style house backing onto Mount Taylor and we signed the papers before I boarded a plane for England. My father was very ill and I went over there for a month. On arrival in England, Peter rang me to tell me that the Company had decided in the end to move to Sydney!

We owned that house for less than a year but 'titivated' it up a bit and managed to make a slight profit. Heaving a sigh of relief we took off for a holiday in Langkawi. The island had only just become popular with tourists. Our Hotel was sparsely occupied but the staff was almost falling over themselves to help make our stay comfortable. We had a great time there but when venturing into the town for lunch one day I found out they only had 'Asian hole in the ground loos' — quite a shock! There was nothing to buy in the shops but of course it has all changed now.

Chapter Six

Moving to Sydney, I then had to find another oncologist and I had carted my mammogram films around with me everywhere. I also had to find a new job and I was offered two positions, one with a litigation/medical practice and the other for a gynaecologist/obstetrician. I chose the latter as I enjoyed seeing the newborns and of course had experience working for a similar practice in Canberra. It was a wise choice. I had a very interesting job working for Dr Cecilia Senior and another new person was recruited a week after I joined. We became great friends and now Jan lives in Perth so we see each other often. My new oncologist was just along the corridor where I worked, which was in the RPA Medical Centre in trendy Newtown. All seemed to be well and I admit to getting a bit blasé about my check-ups. I was also tested for endometrial cancer as I was at risk of that too. In those days they didn't take into account the high risk of ovarian cancer with BRCA 2 patients.

We bought a house in Sydney in beautiful Vaucluse, and I was in seventh heaven. I loved Sydney, enjoyed my job and our house with its huge swimming pool, and a view of the Opera House and Bridge. We did quite a few alterations and were feeling very settled. Then again everything changed; our lives seemed to be always on the move. Peter was asked to run the European office and we had to move over to Europe. I was not happy and very fed up. Peter's boss took us out to lunch at my favourite Balmoral Beach Restaurant to try and win me over. It didn't work! However, being a dutiful wife, off we went. I did, however, manage to get a return ticket back to Australia every year.

Chapter Seven

Peter chose to live in England rather than in mainland Europe, with an office south of London in Guildford. This was handy for both Heathrow and Gatwick airports. Claire had already left Australia to work overseas in London for a while so we saw her often and then Victoria followed. We let the house to a delightful American family whom we became friendly with. They looked after it beautifully and each year I came back and had coffee with Cynthia in 'my own' house!

Again I had to find another oncologist, which was quite easy as I was working as a locum medical secretary in Guildford. I carried on with annual mammograms and all was well. I loved working in Mount Alvernia Hospital and for the private rooms nearby. I also did a couple of locums at the new Nuffield Hospital in Guildford but Mount Alvernia was very special. My breast cancer was just pushed into the background and I only really thought about it when I had my check-ups. I certainly didn't think I was at risk of further disease after such a long time. I hadn't realised how much at risk someone with the BRCA gene was.

Peter and I were living in very pleasant rental houses in Surrey during this time but I missed my own house, so we decided to buy a weekend property. Not being very keen on small low-ceilinged dark cottages, we fell in love with a late Georgian house in Dorset. It had high ceilings, was in the middle of a pretty village and had 7 bedrooms! It had been built many centuries beforehand but had burnt down in 1865 and then re-built. Some remnants of the very old house still remained including very thick walls and an inglenook fireplace. It was across the road from the 800 year old village church and was quite delightful. Also it was only 5 miles from my old favourite town, Dorchester. The little stream called 'The Piddle' ran through our garden, complete with a 'Monet' style bridge!

Victoria came to stay and chose the very top bedroom for herself but sadly Claire never saw it. She had fallen in love with a New Zealand doctor whom she met in a pub in London and they both went back to Auckland. It was another of life's co-incidences as Andrew was born two months before Claire and we had the same GP. I think fate had a hand there! The house was so big; I managed to find a very high-class second-hand curtain shop to solve my dilemma in furnishing it. Thank heavens as the ceilings were very high and so were the windows. The curtains were floor length and beautiful. We sent for our furniture from Australia, which had been in store, thinking we would be there for a long time.

I loved the house, with its AGA cooker and old flagstone floor in the kitchen. I designed a pretty porch for it, as the façade was very 'flat.' I also planted masses of roses in the garden. I arranged for our builders to carve out a terrace at the rear of the house, as a grassy bank soared up from the back of the house. There was no flat area suitable for outdoor seating until that was completed. Odd bushes had been planted here and there in the lawn and I removed them, opening up a pretty vista with the old stables and high stone wall. Sadly we only owned the house for a couple of years as a French firm bought Peter's Australian company and he decided to retire. It was a shame we couldn't live there longer but both girls being overseas made it imperative we moved back 'down under.' Victoria had recently returned to live in Australia. We still have very many friends in the village and in Dorchester and are fortunate to return there every year.

The house in Dorset

Chapter Eight

We then had a dilemma, Claire was in NZ and about to marry Andrew, so we decided instead of returning to Sydney, we would move across to New Zealand, but to Auckland this time. The couple that had been renting our Vaucluse house wanted to buy it so we agreed. In retrospect we should have kept renting it, as prices in Sydney soared after that. We moved to Campbell's Bay on Auckland's North Shore, where we bought a house on top of the cliffs. I watched the America's Cup race sailing right in front of me whilst Peter was out on the water, acting as a Course Marshall. A year later Victoria was married in a lovely old wooden church in Devonport and we held the wedding reception in a marquee in our cliff-top garden.

During this time, I had annual mammograms, which I chose to do privately and I think that probably saved my life. My check-ups were with the North Shore Hospital and the fact that I had the BRCA 2 gene was rather skipped over. I was, however, given one good piece of advice and that was to have a hysterectomy and oophorectomy (removal of my ovaries etc.) so I had that carried out. I had no idea I was at such a risk of another cancer as I had been so diligent having check-ups from the time I was first diagnosed in 1986. I definitely became very complacent and never expected bad news.

I didn't work but did voluntary work for the local hospice and enjoyed gardening there. New Zealand is a wonderful country for gardeners. We also started up the Auckland equivalent of the British NADFAS organisation (Fine Arts Society) and were delighted when it became very well subscribed and popular.

We lived in Campbell's Bay for a few years, and then downsized to a smaller townhouse in Takapuna in Auckland. From there we could see all the ships entering the harbour and also the waves breaking on the beach close by. It was very convenient and perfect for us. Claire's husband had to complete 2 years overseas whilst completing his Fellowship exams and the first year was in London, Ontario. The second year was in Perth and they decided to stay there.

In March 2011, it was my 70th birthday and Peter's brother and wife flew from England to Sydney and so we joined them over there. We had a very pleasant week, celebrating my birthday and we stayed in Kings Cross. Peter took me to see Frankie Valli 'The Jersey Boys' at the theatre and it was a fantastic and happy time. Sadly storm clouds before the rain!

Chapter Nine

On my return, I had my annual mammogram in the Breast Centre and was asked to return the next day, which was very unusual. The first radiologist thought the films were fine but the second one, who always checked the reports, noticed I had a lobular cancer in the same area in the left upper quadrant, as the first breast lump back in 1986.

It was a terrible shock, as I certainly wasn't expecting this! At first I felt I had been given a death sentence as it had spread, affecting my lymph glands. I was then referred to an oncologist and a breast surgeon. A double mastectomy was performed as I felt that gave me a better chance of survival. I was in hospital for a couple of days and the surgeon decided he needed to remove more lymph nodes so again I had more surgery. I then went in for a reconstruction with silicone implants. These have had a bad history but the new silicone ones are I am assured, fine. This involved having expanders, which are assessed regularly, to stretch your chest and some weeks later I was back in hospital to have the implants inserted. All went well but I should have asked for my nipples to be tattooed or something as when I did eventually think about that, the cost was over $3000 and quite ridiculous! I bought 'stick on' ones but fail to use them. I have got used to not having them. I had lymphatic drainage performed by a specialised physiotherapist and was advised to wear the special arm support and flight socks when traveling for more than a few hours. This is particularly important on plane journeys and long car or coach travel. Breast cancer patients are more at risk of blood clots. I was taught how to do my lymphatic drainage exercises and also went to a special physiotherapist trained in the drainage technique. This certainly helps the arm from becoming too swollen.

Some people are quite happy to use prophylactic inserts in their bras but I hated the flat-chested look and was very glad I had the reconstruction. It's a personal choice. When you get a diagnosis like this, you tend to feel very 'alone' which is only natural. It's your own personal fight for life and once you get to grips with it, then you are ready to fight. I thought about it one night and then decided that it wasn't going to define me. There was no point getting all gloomy and sad, as it would make everyone else's life miserable. Once I came to that conclusion, I was ready to deal with it. I feel a positive outlook certainly helps. People often put on a 'concerned' voice and ask '*how are you?*' in sepulchral tones. There is no need to be like that, after all no one knows when their time is up. Often creaking doors like myself last longer than someone who may suddenly lose their life in an accident. We just don't know so it's important to live one's life to the fullest each and every day.

At the age of 60, we had bought an old house in Umbria in Italy not long after we moved back to Auckland, as we really missed Europe. We loved it and had many visitors from the UK and NZ over the ten-year period we owned it. We spent every winter there, a period of 5 or 6 months. We got to know our local villagers and made many great friends there. We joined the Mediterranean Garden Society too so loved seeing so many beautiful gardens in both Tuscany and Umbria. My check-ups were annually so there was no problem in that regard. If I had needed to I could have been checked in either Italy or back in the UK.

These checks were undertaken in Auckland and I had been put on Letrazole, which is a chemotherapy drug. However, I wasn't sure I was having the best advice in Auckland so asked my son in law (a doctor) if we could see someone in Perth when we were there on our regular visits. I was fortunate to see Professor Arlene Chan, whom I think is one of the best oncologists in Australia. After a scan and blood test. She said, if I were **her** patient she would put me on IV chemotherapy, as I was a young, fit 70 year old. As we were departing for our usual 5-6 months sojourn in Italy the next morning, I decided against that and to go with the Auckland oncologist. Not a clever move. The problem with breast cancer is that you don't initially feel ill. It's hard to believe you have this invasive lump inside you.

In retrospect, I should have gone for the chemotherapy that had been suggested but I was far too worried about losing my hair. I had worked in Oncology in Canberra in the early 80s and seen patients losing not only their hair but also their lives. I probably knew too much about it. I also remember the patients wearing a shower cap laden with ice cubes which the nurses had found out seemed to stop them losing their hair. One guy even had a bag made to cover his beard; he was delighted when at the end of treatment, he still had it! How silly to put losing one's hair ahead of saving your life, but then many women do! Our hair defines us; losing our hair isn't the worst thing to happen, not with modern wigs. I also didn't want to miss our wonderful summer in Italy, as we loved it so much. It's a case of wanting your cake and eating it!

It's as well we don't know what is ahead of us!

Our wedding day March 1969

Chapter Ten

We therefore went back to Italy and enjoyed another glorious summer there before returning to Takapuna. We had a very enjoyable social life in Umbria with lunches under the wisteria-clad pergola and visiting friends we had made, mainly through the Mediterranean Garden Society. I suffered quite a bit from fatigue and had afternoon 'siestas' but soon learnt I had to pace myself. The Italian lifestyle is good too and we loved living off the fresh produce we bought in the local market.

We then had a long discussion and decided that it was ridiculous to live in New Zealand when both daughters and our five grandchildren were all in Australia. Another move was on the cards! I have almost lost count of the number of times we have moved, in fact I think we have owned 10 houses and moved approximately 25 times at least! I loathe living in rental properties. I like my own things around me, my paintings on the wall and I hate rental agreements, which disallow you to hang pictures! We missed seeing the grandchildren, and as Claire was staying permanently in Perth whilst Andrew was building up his practice there, we decided to move near them. Victoria's husband was GM of luxury hotels and they moved around quite a bit, mostly in NSW and tended to only be a year or two in each place, so we chose Mandurah. We had stopped here a few years prior to this whilst on a trip around Western Australia in a motor home and liked it.

Umbrian Hills

When we moved from NZ to live in Western Australia in 2014, I became a patient of Arlene Chan and I was put back on Tamoxifen, which initially worked well. Then scans and a blood test (CA 153) showed that my tumour marker level had sadly gone up. I had various CT scans, an MRI and whilst in Auckland had a PET scan. I hated the Bone Scans, as I was always worried about the result. For a few years things were fine and then metastases (secondaries) started showing up in my spine and in the pelvic area. I had no pain by the way all the time I was having these scans. The blood tumour marker level shows if the cancer is not responding to treatment. *Letrazole* had caused a few side effects, but then it stopped working. I then went onto *Everolimus*, plus another drug, *Exemestane*, but that had nasty side effects including mouth ulcers. These drugs are called aromatase inhibitors. The old remedy of *Bonjela* gel for mouth ulcers didn't help but I found that there was a good paste for them called '*Kenalog*.' All drugs have side effects so it's whether you can cope with them or not. Some work well for other people and we all have differing reactions to the drugs.

Dodi's Beach Mandurah still with my own hair!

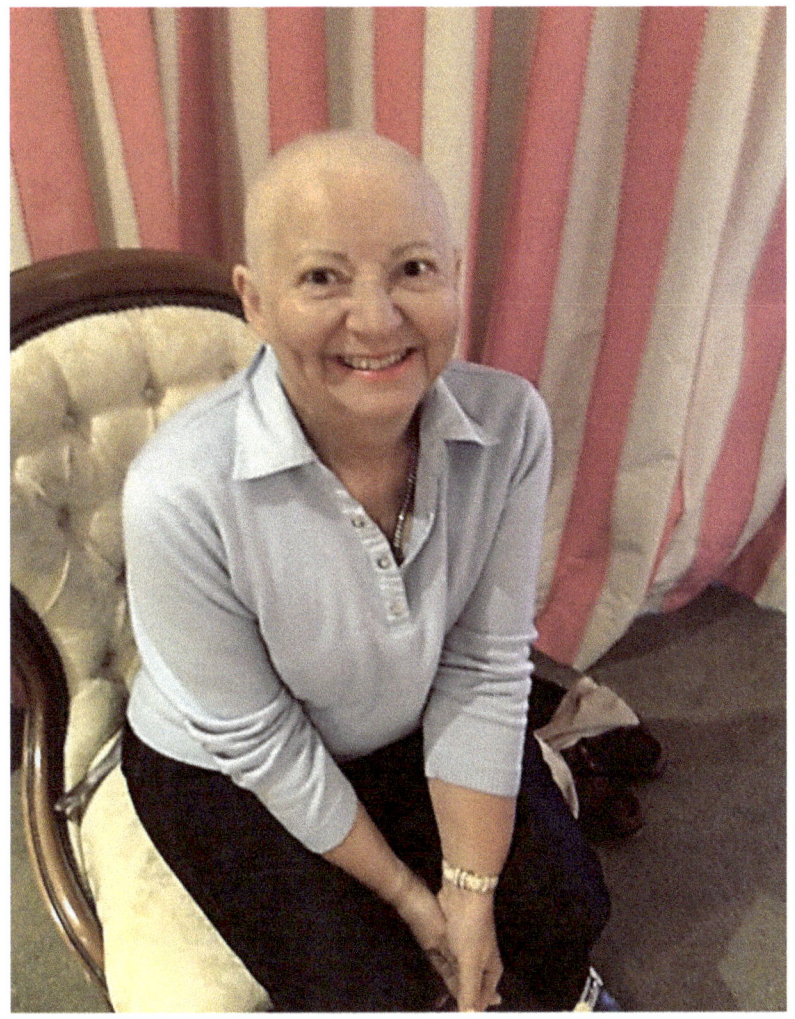

My hair has all gone!

After that I went onto *Fulvestrant* injections; two at once in the buttocks. This involves bending over and two nurses simultaneously injecting the drug. A friend of mine has been on this drug for about 4 years and doing extremely well on it but after a time it stopped working for me. It was also a bit of a nuisance when we went overseas. We had to find a couple of hospitals that could give me the injections. They initially wanted me to see a consultant first but we managed to avoid what was a totally unnecessary appointment. Arlene Chan had sent them a referral anyway. We were in Europe for a couple of months and arranged our itinerary around these appointments. I had the first one in Dorset County Hospital and the second in Bury St Edmunds in Suffolk in the UK. Both were carried out very efficiently but cost over $1000 each. The nurses were used to doing one injection at a time and they thought it must be unpleasant to have it my way but I persuaded them it was much better to get it over and done with! I think I showed them how to do it better and more efficiently the Australian way! One thing I did suffer from were mouth ulcers and I was advised to take Kenalog which is a sort of paste and that helped significantly.

After some months, *Fulvestrant* also stopped being effective so I went onto IV chemotherapy. I decided against the cold cap (the modern equivalent of the shower cap and ice cubes). It took twice as long as the normal chemo session, it is said that the brain feels as if it is frozen, and is very uncomfortably cold! I had a drug to stop me feeling nauseous followed by the chemo. Initially it took a couple of hours but I requested that we stop the anti-nausea drug, as I didn't feel ill at all. We managed to get the time down to an hour. I had had my eyebrows and eyeliner tattooed a few weeks prior so that I would not look quite so 'bare' when my hair fell out, which of course it did. At first I noticed hair on my pillow and in the shower, then my mixed dark and silver hair turned completely white. Probably what happened was that the dark hair fell out first leaving the snowy white to fall out later. I became completely bald (everywhere!) It's a form of a Brazilian without having to shave! It was getting close to Christmas when I had the first chemo so Peter and I visited a fantastic wig emporium, 'Curly Sue's' in Morley in Perth. The women in there were so helpful and knew how to fit the wig so it felt secure. I had a couple of 'welts' removed and was very happy with my wig. It was synthetic and I had a wig block to keep it on and to use when I washed the wig. That was easy when I was at home with the Perth climate as it dried very quickly. However, when we went away, I had to wash it and leave it perched on a towel on a heated towel rail in hotels! It really is wonderful to have a very good wig to keep up your spirits. It was the best thing we could have done. I tried wearing a turban but looked dreadful in one. I wanted a swimming cap to wear in my Aqua-aerobic class and found some beautiful 60's style petal ones on a website in China. It was much admired when I wore it! Mine was a gorgeous turquoise blue but they were available in many other colours.

Wearing my wig on holiday in Wales

I had a small nodule on my neck and it was decided to give me radiotherapy for 5 or 6 weeks. I had to travel up from Mandurah to Subiaco in Perth for this, which necessitated two train rides. I decided to go to a lovely coffee shop each morning so that I had something to look forward to each day. A couple of times a friend came with me and I met my daughter and grandchildren another day. The treatment was fine, except I had to wear what I call a cage and they call a mask! It fitted tightly onto my face so I got them to cut out a tiny bit to give me a bit less pressure. I did get used to it but some patients need sedation, as it is quite claustrophobic! The treatment only lasts such a short time and I did suffer some fatigue. It also feels incredibly tight. Again radiotherapy doesn't hurt! It is important to know if you are going to wear a mask and the staff are incredibly kind and helpful. They guide you and show you exactly what will happen. If it worries you, then sedation is the answer.

I did slather myself in cold cream, which helped and there was one day when I had finished treatment when my skin felt very hot and I pressed a cold, wet flannel on the area. You are given plenty of advice and the staff at the Genesis Cancer unit were wonderful. Next year there will be a Genesis clinic for patients in Mandurah, which is something I would have liked!

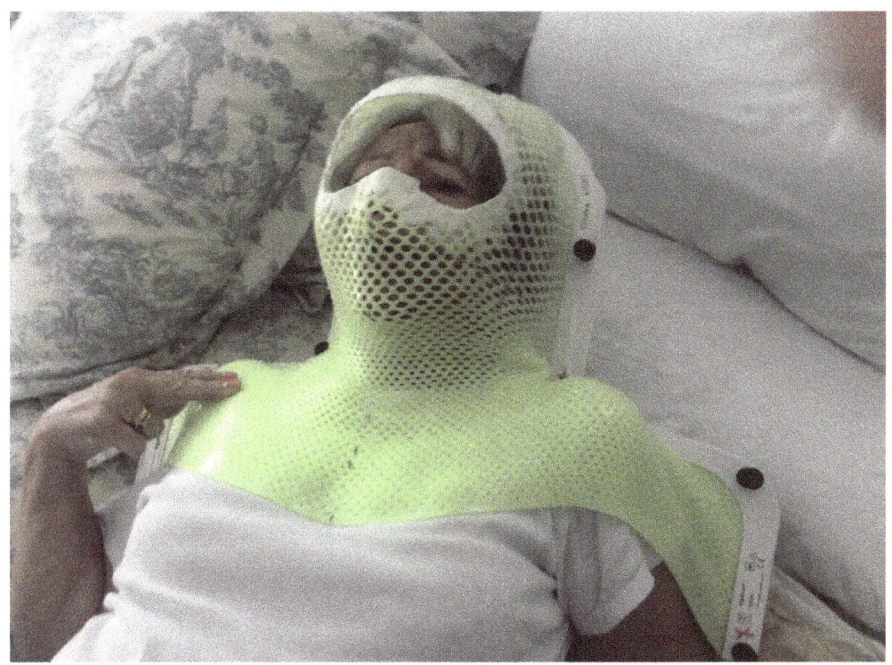

**Demonstrating the mask/cage at home
after I had finished radiotherapy!**

I am now on a regime of chemotherapy drugs and vitamins. My drugs are *Capecitabine* and I take 3 in the morning together with vitamins D and B6 plus the other medications I am on and then 2 more pills in the evening. The side effects with me are occasional diarrhoea and I cannot eat my favourite spicy Indian foods. If I have more than 3 episodes I have to stop taking the next chemo tablets. It mustn't be doubled either so it is just missed out completely. That so far, has only happened once.

I also have very dry hands and the soles of my feet are a dull red and very dry and flaky. I have found a good cream which my GP recommended which is *Calmurid*, which tends to be absorbed into the skin better than most creams. I also sometimes get a watery eye but am feeling really good on this treatment and no longer have a rest in the afternoon. It is 7 years since I first had this particular lobular cancer and every day is a bonus, thanks to the advanced medical care we enjoy in Australia.

I enjoy going to aqua classes for my exercise and I am a writer and have had a couple of books published; one is my autobiography *What a Life*! and the other a novel set in Italy called *A Villa in Umbria* available on Amazon.

So far the side effects are not too difficult to cope with. We are all different and what suits one patient can be detrimental to others.

My hair just growing back and quite curly

Other friends haven't had very good experiences. One friend of mine went to her GP in the UK and showed her the puckering around her nipple. This is a classic example of breast cancer and it is even thought that the famous Mona Lisa painting displays those symptoms. Her GP dismissed it and she had to return two or three times before getting referred for a mammogram. Of course she had breast cancer. She is fortunate to be still alive. Thank our lucky stars we live in Australia!

Now it is 7½ years since I found out I had lobular cancer and it's a question of keeping me alive. So far so good! I had a boyfriend 50 years ago in Ireland, and he subsequently moved to the US. He is a radiologist and checked the mammograms on the CDs I sent him. He could see the cancer, but only **just,** on the previous mammogram a year before it was discovered. It was hard to detect but I was fortunate it wasn't missed on the second viewing in Auckland and if only they had found it the year before.

When you have a diagnosis like mine, time can't stand still. I intend to enjoy every moment I can. Don't despair if you have just been diagnosed. I am living proof that we can lead normal lives with metastatic cancer. Try not to listen to uninformed people, just to your oncologist. We get so many well-meaning items of advice, mainly unrelated to our particular cancer, and 'quack cures.' I am a believer in conventional medicine as it has served me well. As I write this, I am feeling very good. There are some wonderful organisations dealing with breast cancer who will give advice and you can meet other people with similar medical conditions. I have found Prof. Chan's group, PYNK, very beneficial, it is for metastatic cancer patients.

The kConFab organisation in Australia and New Zealand collects tissue from cancer patients and they have been gathering information from patients etc. and collect all this data for research. This is an important organisation and traces the BRCA 1 and BRCA2 genes in families.

Marianne Cable Beach 2018

Other books by this author:

What a Life!

A Villa in Umbria

About the Author

First being diagnosed with breast cancer in 1986, Marianne managed to travel extensively despite ongoing treatment. Together with husband Peter, who was a naval officer and helicopter pilot, they moved to New Zealand for a quieter lifestyle. Both daughters finished their education there. After relocating to Australia they decided to buy an old villa in Umbria which they had for ten years, restoring it and creating a garden with a pool. They enjoyed using the villa as a base to go travelling in Europe and South Africa. After the second cancer was diagnosed in 2011, they moved to Perth to be nearer their daughters and five grandchildren.

www.ingramcontent.com/pod-product-compliance
Lightning Source LLC
Chambersburg PA
CBHW042122100526
44587CB00025B/4152